# Ender's Game:
## *A Reader's Guide*
## *to the Orson Scott Card*
## *Novel*

ROBERT CRAYOLA

# CONTENTS

# INTRODUCTION

Welcome to *Ender's Game: A Reader's Guide to the Orson Scott Card Novel.* This guide will expand your knowledge and understanding of *Ender's Game*, challenging you to think about its deeper levels of meaning, and helping you clarify any confusing aspects of the text. I will be revealing all major details of the book, so if you don't want spoilers, go and read the book first.

*Ender's Game* has become a bestselling science-fiction book, not just for young adults as the book was originally marketed, but for adults as well. Let's try to discover why that is. We'll begin by taking a brief look at the author, Orson Scott Card.

**AUTHOR:** Orson Scott Card was born August 24, 1951 in Washington state. He grew up in California, Arizona, and Utah, serving as a missionary for the Church of Jesus Christ of Latter-day Saints, popularly known as Mormons. Highly influenced by both his Mormon upbringing and his reading, he cites Isaac Asimov's Foundation novels as the spark that turned his attention to science fiction. He says that the idea for the battleroom in *Ender's Game* came to him while he was still a teenager.

After returning from a missionary trip to Brazil, Card began writing for a theater group as well as short story magazines. He worked for a time as an editor until success from his novels in the early 1980s allowed him to devote himself to freelance writing. *Ender's Game*, published first as a short story, was released as an expanded novel in 1985 to popular and critical success, winning both the Hugo and Nebula awards, the most prestigious awards in science fiction. The Ender series would be expanded to include numerous books, short stories, comics, and a movie in 2013.

Aside from his fiction, Card is perhaps somewhat infamous for his criticisms of gay marriage, sparking boycotts of his works from some LGBT groups.

# THE ELEMENTS OF LITERATURE

**WHAT TYPE OF NOVEL IS THIS?:** Let's start looking at *Ender's Game* itself. We're going to examine many of its components, but before we do that, let's find out what *kind* of a book this is. It has been marketed as a teen novel, and it can be seen that way. It also fits into the military science fiction genre. In fact, more than anything, it reminds me of Robert Heinlein's novels, particularly *Starship Troopers* (the alien enemy is even described as bug-like, like Heinlein's aliens) and his juvenile novels. On top of all this, *Ender's Game* is a *Bildungsroman* – a novel that shows a character or characters as they come of age, transitioning from childhood to adulthood. We begin following the main character, Ender, at age six, and he is quickly forced to grow up whether he wants to or not.

**STRUCTURE:** Ender's game is divided into fifteen chapters and has a standard novel length of about 230 pages.

**SETTING:** Setting is the time and place of a story. The time is the future, most likely the 22nd century. We know that it is at least eighty years since the last war against the aliens. The events take place in several locations. The book begins with Ender on the East Coast of the United States. He goes to Battle School, located in the asteroid belt between Mars and Jupiter, and also the Command Center of the International Fleet, far away from the Solar System. Near the end of the book Ender goes to a new colony planet, and then to travel throughout the galaxy.

**NARRATOR AND P.O.V.:** Although we occasionally see things from the perspective of Ender or the other characters, the book is told in the *third-person omniscient* perspective. This means that the narrator can see everything in the story. We mainly follow Ender, but we also move across vast distances to see what is happening on Earth and elsewhere.

**TENSE:** The book is written using the *past tense*.

**TONE:** The tone is how the story feels. *Ender's Game* has a serious, dry tone, occasionally interrupted with dark humor. There is the intensity of a thriller as the war with the aliens draws nearer.

**PLOT:** We'll go over the story in more detail when we do the chapter summaries, but let's get a general outline of the story first. *Ender's Game* is the story of Andrew Wiggin, aka Ender, as he is recruited by the International Fleet to participate in a series of training exercises ("games") at Battle School to prepare him to fight an alien threat known as the buggers. The adults at Battle School present him with increasingly difficult challenges to prepare his mind, but at the loss of Ender's peace of mind. Ender is finally taken to Command School where he learns to command other soldiers in space battles. He is given his "final examination," only to learn that he has been fighting real battles, and that the aliens have been destroyed.

While this has been taking place, Ender's brother and sister have manipulated events on Earth to avert a war. But Ender cannot return home – he is too valuable a player in international politics. He goes instead with his sister to a new colony on a planet formerly held by the aliens. He governs until he discovers a cocoon left by the aliens and a message that is sent into his mind. He learns that the aliens weren't the threat humanity thought they were, and he vows to travel the galaxy until he finds a place for the cocoon to hatch and the aliens to be reborn.

**PROTAGONIST:** The protagonist, or main character, is Andrew Wiggin, known more often simply as Ender.

**ANTAGONIST:** The antagonist is the person or force that opposes the protagonist. There are many characters who antagonize Ender – the bullies Bonzo and Stilson, for instance – but the larger threats come from Ender's brother Peter and the adult world (the International Fleet) that manipulate Ender and do their best to destroy him.

**CONFLICT:** Ender faces conflict throughout the book. He struggles with bullies (Stilson, Peter, Bonzo). He struggles to be his best at Battle School. And he struggles against the adults who would manipulate him and destroy his peace of mind through mental and physical exhaustion.

**CLIMAX:** The climax is the point of greatest tension in the book, the time when the protagonist will either defeat his challenges or be destroyed by them. The climax in *Ender's Game* occurs when Ender is given his "final examination" (really the final battle with the buggers) in Chapter 14.

**RESOLUTION:** The resolution is how the story resolves after the climax has passed. The book's final chapter is devoted to Ender's travel to a new colony planet and his discovery of the alien cocoon left behind, leading to his departure for further travel to find a new home for the aliens. He has reunited with his sister, made peace with his brother, and paved the way for the future inhabitants on the colony planet.

**THEMES:** Themes are the issues the author chooses to highlight through the use of story. Some of the themes in *Ender's Game* include:

*The rights of the individual vs. the needs of society* — Many individual rights are ignored or abused in the militant culture of the novel.

*The ends vs. the means used to achieve those ends* — Connected to the rights of individuals, we witness many abuses by the powers that be in order to save humanity. Children are murdered. Should this be allowed if it will save the human race?

*Compassion and forgiveness* — Ender is a compassionate character forced to do violent and horrible things. He learns forgiveness for his tormentors and his brother, even for the despised aliens. It's possible he may even learn to forgive himself.

*How roles shape personality* — Many characters find themselves changing based on the position they play in the system. Ender changes once he's put in Battle School. His brother and sister change when they wear the anonymous internet masks of "Demosthenes" and "Locke." Personality and character always changes when people find themselves in new roles or positions.

# CHARACTERS

Let's take a look at the characters in the book in the approximate order that they make their appearance.

**ENDER (ANDREW WIGGIN)** – Ender is the main character in the book. He is six years old at the start, the youngest of three children, and we follow him to his early twenties. He is exceptionally intelligent and quickly recruited by the International Fleet to take part in their war games. They believe he may have the skill to defeat the "buggers." Ender genuinely wants to do good and not hurt people, but through the manipulations of adults he is made to do violence.

**VALENTINE WIGGIN** - Valentine is Ender's older sister by two years. She cares deeply for Ender and is one of the few people who can see how Peter tries to hurt Ender. She writes online under the name "Demosthenes" to help shape the world political situation. Like Ender, she is very intelligent and a skilled writer. After the war is over she will emigrate with Ender to a new colony planet and write a history of the war.

**PETER WIGGIN** – Peter is the oldest of the Wiggin children, two years older than Valentine and four years older than Ender (thus ten years old at the start of the book). He is a cruel manipulator. As he matures, he develops an interest in politics and enlists Valentine to help him write and influence others. He writes under the name "Locke." After the war he will gain political control on Earth.

**ENDER'S PARENTS** – Ender's parents play only a minor role in his life. They lack a close connection to their son and can't comprehend what their children are really involved with.

**COLONEL HYRUM GRAFF** – Graff is a high-ranking official in the International Fleet. He recruits Ender, observes and manipulates him. He uses rough tactics and genuinely wants Ender to win. After the war he will be put on trial for his actions, and acquitted.

**STILSON** – Stilson is a bully who gangs up on Ender with other boys when Ender is still on Earth. Ender fights back and hurts Stilson badly. Later, Ender will learn that he actually killed Stilson.

**MISS PUMPHREY** – Ender's teacher on Earth.

**MAJOR ANDERSON** – A subordinate to Colonel Graff at Battle School. He often questions some of Graff's harsh tactics to train Ender, but when Graff is on trial at the end, Anderson testifies in his defense.

**DAP** – A teacher at Battle School. He is one of the few hospitable people to the newly arrived students.

**MICK** – Mick is an older student at Battle School. He sits with Ender and warns him. Ender dislikes his attitude.

**BERNARD** – On the flight to Battle School, Ender is bothered by Bernard. Lashing out, Ender throws Bernard and breaks his arm. Bernard bullies Ender until they reach a kind of truce through Alai. Later Ender will realize that Bernard still resents him.

**SHEN** – Shen is Ender's first real friend at Battle

School. They share Bernard as a common enemy.

**ALAI** – Alai is a talented strategist at Battle School. His best friend is Bernard. He respects Ender and will prove to be a good friend in the long run.

**GENERAL LEVY** – A minor character at Battle School who questions Graff's methods.

**BONZO MADRID** – A major bully at Battle School. He leads Salamander army and is Ender's commander for a brief time. He resents Ender's superior skill and later fights him in the shower. Ender wins the fight and kills Bonzo, but he isn't sure of this until later.

**PETRA ARKANIAN** – The only girl in Salamander army. She befriends Ender and proves her loyalty to him by warning him about the conspiracy against him.

**ROSE THE NOSE** – Leader of the Rat army. When he sees Ender's true ability, he allows him some freedom to do what he wants in battle.

**DINK MEEKER** – Dink heads a toon (army subdivision) in Rat army. He is a loyal friend to Ender and warns him about Bonzo's planned attack.

**MAJOR IMBU** – Imbu explains the computer's "thought process" to Colonel Graff, and has a better understanding of it than many characters.

**DR. LINEBERRY** – She works at Valentine's school as a counselor or psychologist.

**BEAN** – When Ender gets his own army, Bean is one of his most talented soldiers. Bean is small, however, and Ender picks on him to make him stronger.

**CARN CARBY** – The commander of Rabbit army. Even though Ender defeats his army, Carby and Ender respect each other.

**FLY MOLO** – Leader of a toon in Ender's Dragon army.

**CRAZY TOM** – A soldier in Ender's Dragon army.

**GENERAL PACE** – Chief of the International Fleet's military police. He is angry at Graff when Bonzo is killed.

**ADMIRAL CHAMRAJNAGAR** – A teacher at I.F. Command School.

**MAZER RACKHAM** – A legendary figure from the last war against the buggers, almost singlehandedly responsible for winning the war. Ender meets him at I.F. Command and is surprised to find him alive. He has traveled through space at high speed to allow him to move through time more slowly (due to relativity), so he is only about sixty years old. He helps Ender in the final days of his "training," when Ender is really fighting the actual aliens.

# GLOSSARY

Like many science fiction and fantasy titles, this book has a great deal of terminology unique to it. Here are a few of the unusual terms that occur in the text.

**ANSIBLE** – An ansible is a device that allows instantaneous communication across the galaxy. It is not subject to the limitations of the speed of light, and is the main method of communication across vast distances by the humans. The aliens seem to have the technology as well, but it seems to be more directly wired into their biology.

**BUGGERS** – This is how the humans refer to the aliens in the novel. In later books Card would refer to the aliens as *Formics*, but they are simply known as buggers (because of their insect-like nature) in this first book.

**DR. DEVICE** – Molecular Destruction Device (hence "M.D. Device"). Used by the humans in space battles.

**ECSTATIC SHIELD** – This is a defense device used in space battles.

**GIRIA** – A type of slang used by students at Battle School.

**HEGEMONY, POLEMARCH, AND STRATEGOS** – The three main ruling parties on Earth.

**STARS** – In the context of the battleroom, stars are obstacles that can block you from your opponent.

**THIRD** – A third child in the family. Since there are negative repercussions for families who have more than two children, "third" is a term carrying a social stigma. Ender is a third.

**TOON** – A subdivision of an army at Battle School. The armies each have one commander who divides the army into toons and assigns a toon leader to each toon.

# CHAPTER SUMMARIES & COMMENTARY

**CHAPTER ONE: "THIRD"** – This first chapter introduces us to Andrew Wiggin, aka "Ender," a six-year-old boy of unusually high intelligence. He lives on Earth in the future. Before we actually get to see him though, there are voices looking on at him. These voices will observe Ender through the book, and Card indicates these voices by using a different font for the text. This is a typographical convention that clarifies the shift in narrative. We'll later learn that these voices belong to officers in the International Fleet, particularly Colonel Graff, but for now they are mysterious.

Ender is having his *monitor* removed. A monitor in the book is a device in the back of the neck, bound to a person's nervous system, that allows others to feel and experience whatever that person is feeling. Monitors are put in children to see if they have potential to join in the fight against the *buggers*. Buggers are the aliens that have had two wars with humanity. Ender has had his monitor in him for three years, one year longer than his brother. Ender is hoping to be accepted by his brother once the monitor is gone. The medical staff tell him that its removal won't be painful, but it is, and Ender nearly dies.

After recovering, he returns to school. He is a little disoriented without his monitor. His teacher, Miss Pumphrey, knows why he's been out and is sympathetic. The students soon figure it out too when they see the band-aid on Ender's neck. They start mocking him, calling him a *third*. This is the chapter title as well. It refers to Ender's place in his birth order. He has an older brother, Peter, and an older sister, Valentine. The government attempts to limit population, and families that have a *third* child must sign away their rights to the child if the government chooses to make use of him or her. We see this is a militant culture, and a lot of individual rights have been lost.

We learn that Ender is very intelligent. He can answer all his teacher's questions if need be, and he figured out a way to send messages between the desk imaging systems. Nevertheless (or because he is seen as teacher's pet), his peers mock him. After class, a boy named Stilson and some others wait to bully Ender. Without a monitor in Ender's neck, Stilson thinks no one will know about the bullying. Ender mocks Stilson for requiring so many others to beat him up. Quickly taking the offensive, Ender kicks Stilson and knocks him down. Then, rather than allowing Stilson to recover, Ender kicks him while he is down and shouts a warning to the others. Although he doesn't want to fight, Ender knows he must set an example or the bullying will continue.

Afterward, Ender cries and thinks, "I am just like Peter." In Ender's mind, being like his sadistic older brother is perhaps the worst thing he can be.

Our first view of Ender in this chapter shows us that

he is good at reasoning, making quick decisions and acting upon them. This is likely why his observers are so interested in him. We also see that he has a good heart, even if his actions don't always appear altruistic. But his tears at the end of this chapter reminds us that this is still a six-year-old boy.

**CHAPTER TWO: "PETER"** – Ender's observers begin this chapter by commenting on his fight with Stilson. There is a mix of pride and fear about what Ender has done, and what will be done to him in the future.

He arrives home and his sister Valentine consoles him about the loss of his monitor. It's like losing a body part. Peter arrives on the scene and sees the monitor is gone. Like the bully Stilson, Peter sees this as an opportunity to torture Ender without observation from outsiders. Because Ender kept his monitor one year longer than Peter, he has a hatred of Ender. He can't understand what they saw in Ender that they didn't see in him.

Peter forces Ender to play a game of "Buggers and Astronauts," a boyish game similar to "Cowboys and Indians." Peter puts a mask on Ender (who will be the bugger), impairing his view. Peter has the advantage in both vision and size, and he presses Ender under his weight. He tells Ender he might just kill him now and say it was an accident. However, Valentine interrupts Peter. She understands Peter well, and believes he wants to be in politics when he's older. She threatens him with a letter she says that she's written, accusing Peter of foul play should she die unnaturally. Whether there is such a letter or not, or whether Peter was only fooling around to demonstrate his power over his siblings, he decides to back down. Peter says that Valentine is Ender's "monitor" now, looking out for him.

Ender's parents arrive home and console him further about the loss of his monitor. Ender cannot tell his parents about Peter.

That night, Ender is lying down and Peter stands over him. Ender thinks he might try to suffocate him with a pillow. Instead, Peter apologizes to Ender and says he loves him. This is so completely at odds with what Peter said earlier that Ender must find it unbelievable. Confused, he cries once again.

**CHAPTER THREE: "GRAFF"** – Even without the monitor in him, Ender's observers keep close watch on him. They know of his fight with Stilson. They are interested in him, but they think his love for his sister Valentine may be a weak link. If he cares for her too much, he won't leave. They need to make him *want* to leave.

The next morning at breakfast Ender is in low spirits. He's worried about what he'll have to face at school that day. The family is all there and they lightheartedly joke like in a sitcom. Then the mood is soured when a man arrives at their front door. He is wearing the uniform of the International Fleet, the military organization operating in outer space. The family had been relieved when Ender's monitor was removed. It seemed to signify they weren't interested in Ender. Now they are worried that they might want him after all.

The man enters their home to speak with Ender and his parents. He informs Ender's parents about the fight with Stilson, and they are disappointed. Ender explains his reasons for beating Stilson so badly – to avoid further confrontations with bullies – and Graff is satisfied with his rationale. It shows that Ender thought the fight through. The officer introduces himself to Ender as Colonel Hyrum Graff, director of primary training at Battle School in the Belt. Observing how Ender would behave without his monitor was the last step in the observation process, and they are sure they want him now. They technically have the right to take him. His parents had to sign him away to the government before he was even born because he is a *third*. However, Colonel Graff doesn't want to *take* Ender. He wants Ender to voluntarily go with him. Graff wants Ender to be an officer, a high-ranking official in the fight against the buggers, and that will only work if Ender wants to go with him. Ender dislikes fighting, but he thinks about being away from Peter for ten years, and there is a part of him that wants to go.

Colonel Graff asks to speak with Ender alone. He tells Ender about what he'll experience, about what it means to leave your life behind on Earth for ten years. Then Graff uses Ender's status as a third to make him feel guilty. He says that Ender's parents will always feel a public shame at having a third. He talks about their religious backgrounds and makes a convincing argument to Ender. He also explains that Ender will be studying and playing war games in zero gravity.

Graff also says that they originally wanted Ender's brother Peter, but they found him too cruel. They thought Valentine might be gentler, but she proved to be too gentle. With Ender they feel they've found just the right middle ground, but they can't be sure until they see him perform. They are looking for a strategic genius on the level of Mazer Rackham, the military commander whose tactics helped win the last war against the buggers, eighty years ago. Graff warns, however, that once Ender leaves with him, there will be no turning back. With all this in mind, Ender agrees to go. He says his goodbyes to his family. Peter makes a lighthearted joke, and Valentine shows she is the closest to Ender, and says she will love him forever.

**CHAPTER FOUR: "LAUNCH"** – Ender's observers at the beginning of this chapter – who we now can guess are the International Fleet, including Colonel Graff – start this chapter by saying that Ender must become a leader. The size of the next war of the buggers means that one commander won't be able to handle all the battles. They talk of their plan to make Ender lose his "sweetness."

At the launch of Ender into space, he's going with twenty other children. He hasn't been allowed to eat for twenty hours before the launch. This is to prevent him from vomiting once he enters the zero gravity of outer space.

Ender is already feeling like an outsider again among the other children. They are joking and laughing with each other. He is alone in his head. He imagines a TV interviewer asking him questions about the launch. As Ender enters the shuttle, he notices that it's designed with no "top" in mind. Once they get into space there will be no gravity, and our normal ideas about direction will be thrown out the window.

Ender sees that Colonel Graff is returning to Battle School with the children. He says that he doesn't normally come to Earth for recruiting. Ender feels momentarily that he has a friend in the colonel.

The launch into space is rough. Ender wonders if something might be going wrong, but that's just part of the process. Children are nauseous, and it's clear why they weren't allowed food beforehand. As zero gravity takes effect, Ender laughs to himself as he imagines Colonel Graff standing on his head. Graff notices Ender's mirth and takes the opportunity to pick Ender out for humiliation. He makes Ender seem like a really smart kid, and the other boys view him as the teacher's pet. A boy in the seat behind Ender repeatedly hits Ender in the head because of this. Unwilling to take the bullying, Ender grabs the boy's arm and hurls him across the room. Ender didn't intend to seriously hurt him, but in the zero gravity his maneuver was more dangerous, and the boy's arm is broken. Graff uses the incident to make Ender feel even more isolated from the others.

Ender talks to Graff alone. He thought he had a friend in Graff, but the colonel is glad to deny this.

When Ender has gone, Graff talks with Anderson, a teacher at Battle School. He tells Anderson that he doesn't like what he has to do, but he'll do it. He wants to produce the best soldiers, that it's their only chance of defeating the buggers. He will do whatever is necessary to make Ender the best, or break him in the process.

We see in Colonel Graff an intelligence on par with Ender.

**CHAPTER FIVE: "GAMES"** – Ender's observers probably look like sadists by this point in the book. Their motivation is a classic case of "the ends justifying the means," and you'll have to decide if you think they're making the right choice. After all, the fate of humanity seems to hang in the balance. People throughout history have suffered far more than Ender for far lesser causes. However that may be, they have decided to take away a large part of Ender's childhood by forcing him into this cold environment.

Ender arrives at Battle School and gets to his bunkroom. He and many others are tightly crammed into a low-ceilinged room. The only bed left is the bottom bunk near the door. Ender knows this is an undesirable location, but he pretends that he wants it. In his bed and locker he discovers his things. They include a suit that resembles a spacesuit (but isn't airtight), and a laser gun of some sort. These will be used in the strategy games the students play.

As Ender examines his things, an adult comes in. He introduces himself to the students as Dap, and calls himself their "mom." He will be like an R.A. (residential advisor) to the students. He gives them basic information about Battle School. Everything has a coded, militant feel, and Dap warns them about going places where they shouldn't be. He is both stern and humorous, saying, "Give me any lip and I'll break your face." He also explains the circular structure of the space station they're in. It spins and the centrifugal force provides gravity.

Ender learns the name of the boy who pushed him on the shuttle, the boy whose arm Ender broke: Bernard. He is French and hates Ender. He is amassing a gang of boys, and Ender says that he is "a Stilson," recalling the boy who bullied him on Earth.

Ender learns more about the games students play. The children are divided into teams with names like Scorpions, Flame, and Tide, and they usually only associate with their team members. There is a great deal of competition, and people constantly keep track of team standings.

While Ender is eating, a boy named Mick sits with him. Mick is about twelve and *not* a leader. He has failed to make anything of himself at Battle School. He warns Ender and has a negative attitude. Ender dislikes him for this, and refuses to absorb his negativity.

There is a good deal of homesickness among the other students. They miss their families, their pets, and Earth. Ender also wants to go home, but he refuses to show weakness and will not let anyone see his tears.

His studies begin and Ender finds them more difficult than on Earth. It's the first time he's struggled with learning in his life. The game room is introduced by Dap. We can imagine the games as a combination of video games and physical activity. Some of the games are familiar to Ender; some are new. He watches the others play and wants to take part himself. They brush him aside, unwilling to give him a chance. He is a newbie and they are sure they can beat him. Ender challenges them and says they are afraid to play him. In order to get rid of him and shut him up, they let him play. He wins two out of three. They are surprised and blame the loss on the machine, citing it as faulty, but Ender knows they are already taking note of him.

Realizing he has an enemy in Bernard and his gang, Ender seeks allies in other bullied students. One such kid is Shen. Bernard mocks his butt. Ender hacks the messaging system in the student desks, and it looks like Bernard is sending humiliating messages to all the students. Bernard suspects Ender, but can prove nothing. Bernard tells Dap, and Dap only embarrasses him further. At the end of the chapter, Shen is sure Ender is behind Bernard's humiliation, and they join forces as friends.

**CHAPTER SIX: "THE GIANT'S DRINK"** – Ender's International Fleet observers begin this chapter by reflecting on previous students, like Ender, who showed great promise, only to fail. This is a standard device in fiction – a character who is either "the chosen one," or about to face an obstacle that *no one else has ever overcome*. One famous example of this is the Arthurian legend, when the young Arthur is the only one able to remove the sword in the stone. But there is concern that

Ender may not be the one to face the buggers, after all. He is stuck with a video game. Furthermore, he has created dissent in his launch group.

For the first time, one of Ender's observers is clearly identified as Colonel Graff. We see that Graff and the others have confidence in Ender, but that the boy could easily fail.

The group of new students enter the battleroom for the first time. This is a more "physical" game and it takes place in zero gravity. It makes use of the gun and suit that Ender found in his locker. Each students is wearing one, and they begin to jump around and test their abilities. Ender is one of the more adventurous students in this, while other students like Bernard and Shen are more cautious. Ender finds that when he pushes off of something, he flies away until he hits something else. You can think of it like the game of pool, but instead of a ball the object moving is a person, and instead of a flat table, it is a three-dimensional space.

Ender notices Alai, Bernard's best friend, and sees that he is also very experimental with his maneuvers. Ender propels himself near Alai, and they try to tricks together, using their bodies to launch each other in unique ways and reflect in mid-air. They seem to get along well, but their friendship is tenuous because of Bernard's hatred of Ender.

They test the guns they've been given and discover that they freeze you in place when you're shot. Taking Shen and Bernard into their confidence, they use their guns to freeze everyone else in the room.

Dap arrives and the other kids complain about being frozen. Unsympathetic, Dap scolds them for not figuring out their guns as quickly as Ender and the other boys. Alai is described as a "bridge" between Ender, Bernard, and Shen, and because of his popularity, Alai is voted launch leader.

In his free time, Ender plays a video game. It features a giant that offers Ender two drinks (what the chapter title refers to). Every time Ender plays and drinks, he dies. He cannot figure out a way past the impossible challenge. Finally, he does something unorthodox: he knocks both drinks over and attacks the giant, accidentally killing him. He has overcome the challenge.

Although Ender has won, he feels he is becoming like Peter. If violence is his only solution, is he that different from Peter after all? The giant's death will foreshadow a real-life murder that Ender unintentionally commits later in the book.

**CHAPTER SEVEN: "SALAMANDER"** – We start to see the strategy that Ender's trainers will employ: Give him a challenge, a difficult situation, and as soon as he solves it, give him an even more difficult problem. Thus Ender will always have to make his skills sharper and think about the bigger picture if he hopes to stay alive.

His observers wonder if they really want Ender in charge of their fleet – they just saw what he did to the giant in the game – but they say that winning is the important thing. This ethical dilemma about the ends justifying the means is at the heart of the novel.

Alai begins this chapter with Ender. He explains how Ender hacked the messaging system. Alai is impressed and wants access to the unique security protection system Ender has developed. Ender is going to show him, but he finds that all his computer access codes have been blocked.

Since Ender has grown comfortable with his launch group, earning their respect and making peace with

Bernard, his observers decide to shake things up. Even though he is not yet seven, they decide to put him in one of the armies: Salamander. It is commanded by Bonzo Madrid, who will prove to be a main antagonist of Ender.

Ender says goodbye to his friends emotionally, then plays his video game again. It has a dreamlike quality as Ender overcomes its challenges, and then tells him, "Death is your only escape." His game is interrupted when he is ordered to report to his new Commander. He is late. As he makes his way to Salamander army's barracks room, he dreams of a life where he doesn't have to fight and kill, and he contemplates what "just living" might be like.

Salamander army is a larger group than his launch group, and Ender finds he is the youngest one there. A girl named Petra Arkanian talks to Ender and describes Salamander army as a bad place to be. Its commander, Bonzo, is annoyed to receive Ender, inconvenienced about receiving such an inexperienced soldier. But there is a pride to the group and they pledge to overcome their new weakness – Ender. As they talk, Petra makes a comment. Bonzo doesn't like the interruption and slaps her across the face. We see that Bonzo has a temper and doesn't have the full respect of his army. Similar to Shen's abuse by Bernard, Ender will take advantage of Bonzo's abuse of Petra to befriend her.

Bonzo doesn't want to train Ender. When they battle, he wants Ender to stay near the entrance gate and do nothing, not even removing his gun. Bonzo mainly wants to trade Ender away to another army.

Petra agrees to train Ender in the mornings when the battlerooms are mostly empty. Ender learns quickly. Even when he goes with his army to practice and he can't participate, he makes notes to himself. Eager for more practice, Ender goes back to his launch group and agrees to train them in his free time with the knowledge he's gathered. Bonzo doesn't like this and orders Ender to stop. But the order can't be enforced. Ender is free to use his free time as he wants. He talks with Ender alone and Ender advises the older boy to change his order publicly to avoid embarrassment. Bonzo can say that allowing Ender to train with his launch group will make him easier to trade away. Bonzo does this soon after. By taking advice from a younger, inexperienced student, Bonzo acknowledges Ender as the superior strategist. If Bonzo was smarter he would train Ender, perhaps put him in charge of a toon (a subgroup in the army). Instead, Bonzo chooses to let Ender raise anger him even more.

When Salamander army actually faces other groups, Ender does nothing. He could prevent a total loss and make the battle a draw, but he follows his orders to the letter, and he knows it makes Bonzo even angrier. Because Ender wasn't actually "killed" in battle, only frozen (he could still move his hands), his score in the standings is unusually high. Rather than change his orders (and admit that Ender was right and should participate), Bonzo tells Ender that the orders remain the same.

Time passes and Ender is now seven. There is no birthday celebration, but he remembers that he is doing all this to save his family from the buggers, especially Valentine. He still can't participate in the real battles, but he learns through observation and the practice battles with his launch group.

Then, during a battle with Leopard army, Ender uses a unique strategy, feigning that he was already shot, and then firing upon the enemy when they thought the battle was over. He turns a loss into a draw – but in doing so he violates Bonzo's orders.

Angrier than usual, Bonzo announces that Ender has been traded to Rat army, and then he punches Ender. But Ender knows that this only makes Bonzo look weaker among his army, and Ender is glad to finally leave Bonzo.

Ender can no longer train with Petra (because she's now in a competing army). Also, to protect himself, he signs up for a martial arts course.

**CHAPTER EIGHT: "RAT"** – Orson Scott Card makes it clear in this chapter that the two speakers discussing and observing Ender are Colonel Graff and Major Anderson. Graff wants to start making the games unfair to Ender, "cheating," so the boy will have to come up with new solutions and think in unconventional ways. Anderson threatens to tell their superiors and get Graff in trouble, and Graff justifies his actions in the interest of human survival. The International Fleet is heading toward the bugger homeworlds for an offensive attack, and Ender needs to be ready when they arrive. It's unclear when that will be at this point in the book. Anderson says that Graff is being hypocritical, that he doesn't like it when Anderson threatens to make life difficult for Graff. Graff counters by saying that Ender is far smarter than him.

Ender joins the Rat army and finds it quite different from Salamander. It is noisier in the sleeping quarters – he had grown used to quiet. The commander of Rat army is known as Rose the Nose. He is Jewish and his real name is Rosen. Rose sends Ender to a toon leader named Dink. Ender meets him and finds him more intelligent than the other boys he's met. Dink has carefully observed Ender, for one thing. He gives Ender this advice: "The more you obey them, the more power they have over you." He's talking about army commanders, but his attitude extends beyond that to include the adults.

Dink is the first to make use of Ender. He lets Ender show Dink's toon the feet-first attack that he's developed. When they go into battle for the first time, Ender is given instructions to attack right away. Instead of instantly being frozen by the enemy, Ender's tactics keep him alive for a while. And Rose the Nose isn't so hard on him after that. Dink starts to make greater use of Ender's strategy.

One day, Ender stays in the battleroom to see what Dink does in there alone. He finds that Dink just floats. They talk and Ender learns that Dink has refused promotion. He thinks the whole war against the buggers is a sham, a means of keeping humanity united and suppressed by the International Fleet. Ender is concerned that Dink may be right, but he finally concludes that the buggers are still a genuine threat.

The next time Ender is a practicing with his launch group, he finds that a lot of the kids aren't there. It turns out they're being bullied into not coming. Ender wants to call the sessions off so no more students are bullied, but Alai won't let him. They go on with the training and students from other armies show up to jeer at them. Ender turns the taunts back on the older boys and a fight breaks out. Ender uses his combat training and skills as a commander to win the fight. The teachers don't discipline Ender and the injuries from the fight are put down as the result of an "accidental collision." Other students hear about the fight, and at the next training Ender has 45 students eager to be trained by him.

Ender plays his video game again, and while looking at a mirror within the game, he sees Peter's face looking back at him. This corresponds to his feeling that he is no better than Peter when he becomes violent.

**CHAPTER NINE: "LOCKE AND DEMOSTHENES"** – Ender's observers begin this chapter wondering how the computer could have inserted Peter's face into the game Ender was playing. The computer is so advanced that it's reasoning is beyond human minds, and it pulled Peter's photo for reasons that Graff and the others can't understand.

This chapter mostly takes place on Earth. Ender is now eight, and Valentine lights a candle for him on his birthday. The Wiggin family is living in Greensboro, North Carolina, in closer proximity to nature in an attempt to make Peter gentler. Instead, Peter has tortured squirrels. Valentine continues to miss Ender. She also knows Peter is still bad underneath, however much his parents and teachers are convinced he's changed. Both Valentine and Peter are very intelligent, and Peter has decided he needs Valentine, specifically her writing skills, to help him manipulate the entire planet.

You must remember that this novel was first published in 1985, when the World Wide Web was not yet in existence. Still, Card was aware of the internet and many people could see that the web was coming. He tries to show this in the novel, and although his conception of it and how people use it is more rigid and formal than it actually came to be, we can understand what he was going for. Essentially, Peter wants Valentine to help him create two people who write political commentary online. Valentine will write as "Demosthenes," named after the ancient Greek orator, and Peter will write as "Locke," named after John Locke, an English philosopher of the Enlightenment. Peter believes Russia is mobilizing for war. There has been a longstanding peace since the bugger wars united humanity against a common enemy, but Peter thinks the war with the buggers may soon be over. Using his convincing rhetoric, and playing on Valentine's desire to help humanity, she agrees to help him for now. She still suspects he is just putting on an act to get what he wants, but she'll keep an eye on him. She thinks, "You're so clever, Peter. You saved your weakness so you could use it to move me now." She's also not sure if what he says isn't partly true after all.

They began to publish things online, on "the nets" as the book refers to it, and they learn quickly, polishing their rhetoric and growing in popularity. They earn followings and are soon paid to write – not in money but in access to networks they couldn't otherwise post to. Valentine doesn't always like what she has to write as Demosthenes, and she is sickened when her father praises her writings (not knowing she wrote it, of course).

Returning to Ender, he is now nine and a toon leader in Phoenix army, commanded by Petra. He finds that he misses the camaraderie he had when he didn't have any command. Now students respect him too much, which distances him from them.

In his video game he is stuck at a place called "The End of the World." He is filled with despair that he'll ever escape from his scenario, in the game or in real life.

Colonel Graff sees that Ender is flailing, and he seeks the help of Valentine. Returning to Earth, he asks her to write Ender a letter, and unlike the previous letters she sent, Graff will allow this letter to make it through to her brother. Graff is smart and able to tell when Valentine is trying to trick him. She doesn't like Graff or what they've done to Ender, but she does want to help him. Graff is most concerned about Ender's feeling that he's becoming like Peter.

Valentine writes the letter. Ender recognizes telltale signs that it's actually from her and not a forgery. Even though he knows they coerced her into writing the letter, if affects him. When he next plays his video game, he kisses the snake, something he'd never considered, and it turns into Valentine and he's able to go forward.

The International Fleet thanks Valentine for her part in helping Ender, and that makes her question her actions even more.

**CHAPTER TEN: "DRAGON"** – Ender's observers note that he's almost been happy recently, but now they have to start challenging and hurting him again. They are preparing to attack the buggers and need him to be ready. Colonel Graff describes the isolation they're creating for Ender as "the loneliness of power."

They call Ender in to speak with him and let him know he'll be commanding an army. He already knew that would happen, but he's surprised to learn he'll be getting Dragon army, since there is no Dragon army. It will be an entirely new army with a lot of inexperienced soldiers. And to make it more difficult for him, he can't trade any of them to other armies. He also cannot train any other army members (as he's been doing) or use his hook outside of regular practice sessions. His hook is a device that lets him maneuver anywhere he wants in the battleroom.

Ender's soldiers are all younger than him. He is hard on them from the beginning, making them dress fast and yelling at them in a manner similar to Graff's harassment of Ender early on. Ender is particularly hard on a small boy named Bean, who is also a gifted student like Ender. He sees a lot of himself in Bean and wonders why he is so hard on him. He doesn't like what he becoming.

Ender sees improvement in the army quickly, and he's showing them everything he can to get them up to speed. He cannot associate with them much out of practice sessions and battles. He must keep his distance, however much he dislikes it. Even when he sees his former friends like Alai, there is a distance now. They joke, but they cannot be friends. They will soon be enemies in battle. Ender feels a newfound strength and coldness, and thinks he is now strong enough to face the teachers. He is starting to take the view that they are his real enemies.

**CHAPTER ELEVEN: "VENI VIDI VICI"** – This title's chapter is a Latin phrase that translates as "I came, I saw, I conquered," and is usually attributed to Julius Caesar. It will relate to the relentless battles Ender endures in this chapter.

His observers at the school take note of Ender's battle schedule. No army has ever had to battle so frequently, but it's largely the decision of the computer. Colonel Graff and the others put a lot of faith in the computer's ability to hone Ender's skill and make him the best, but they also want to make sure he isn't a broken boy by the time his training is done.

We also learn of events on Earth: Russia and the U.S. are drifting apart as an end to the bugger wars approaches. They seem to allude to Valentine and Peter, in their net identities as "Demosthenes" and "Locke," who are stirring things up. It's ironic that it is Ender's siblings who are doing this, but also ironic because they don't always believe the position they are endorsing in their writings.

Ender's Dragon army faces its first battle against Rabbit army. Ender's army wins. Carn Carby is commander of Rabbit army and he congratulates Ender after the battle. Although they won, Ender is hard on his soldiers, pointing out where they could have done better. He doesn't want to lose a single battle.

Ender can now eat with the other army leaders in the commanders' mess hall. He has a high rank in the standings from that first battle, and Dink (who finally accepted a command position) congratulates him. Ender is a little cocky, and intends to keep getting victories.

Over the next week, his army fights a battle every day. This is very unusual, and Ender knows it. Nevertheless, he is able to win every time. Even when he has a to fight two battles in one day, against Bonzo Madrid and with the game stacked against him, he still manages to pull off a victory (although with heavy losses). Ender has quickly moved to the top in the rankings. He has also created a lot of enemies in the process. His defeat of Bonzo was especially humiliating. Ender knows he has insulted the Spaniard's honor.

To insure future victories, Ender confides in Bean, the small boy he picked on before. He knows Bean is the smartest soldier he has, and he wants him to train a special group of students to do completely unexpected things. Bean agrees, happy to finally get some respect from Ender.

**CHAPTER TWELVE: "BONZO"** – Colonel Graff finds himself in the spotlight at the beginning of this chapter. He is starting to seem obsessed in his manner of molding Ender into a tool to defeat the buggers, and military police is taking an interest. General Pace, chief of I.F. military police, interviews Graff. They know that a group of children hostile to Ender are planning to beat him up, possibly killing him in the process. Graff doesn't want to interfere. He can't let Ender think that he can be "saved," but he has faith that Ender will overcome any attack. General Pace isn't so certain, and he threatens Graff with a court martial if Ender is seriously hurt.

As Ender's relentless series of battles continue, he keeps coming up with new tactics, along with Bean. They use "deadlines," thin twine that is virtually invisible, to propel them around the battleroom faster than anyone's ever seen.

Because of his success, Ender is facing serious threats from students outside the battleroom. He and his army are still mainly composed of smaller kids. It seems that Salamander army (led by Bonzo Madrid, remember) is particularly threatening. Petra and Dink warn Ender, and his troops take the threat seriously, but he's still a little lax with precautions.

One day after a battle, Ender goes to the shower alone. Bonzo, Bernard, and several other boys cut off his exit. Knowing he's outnumbered, Ender uses Bonzo's sense of pride to make him fight Ender alone. He also turns up the hot water on the shower so his skin will be slippery. They fight and Ender is able to slip away from Bonzo and seriously hurt him. Dink takes Ender away and teachers come to check on Bonzo. Ender has a uncanny feeling that Bonzo didn't feel his last kick – the Spaniard had a vacant look in his eyes. Later, we'll learn that he's been killed, as had Stilson back on Earth. Ender is unaware of the extent of his own power. Ender also notes that help only comes when the fight is *over*.

Thoroughly exhausted from the battleroom and then the fight with Bonzo, Ender is almost ready to give up when he gets an order for another battle that evening. And to make it worse, he will be fighting two armies at the same time. He tells Bean and the others. They are confident, and Ender is ready to try anything if the teachers are intent to throw out the rules.

They use a battle formation, something they don't usually do. In the chaos of the fight, Ender bypasses normal protocol by passing through his enemy's gate, which the battleroom recognizes as a victory. Major Anderson is mad at Ender for using this tactic, but Ender doesn't care. He knows they are toying with him and he's ready to do the same back to them.

Afterward, Ender learns that Bean and his other best soldiers are being sent to other armies. But Ender doesn't care at this point. He's sick of their mind games and doesn't care what happens.

Then, to Ender's surprise, Colonel Graff tells him he is being sent to Command School. Not only is Ender younger than usual for this, but he is bypassing Pre-command school.

He leaves with Graff in a shuttle. They head to Earth, where Ender will briefly stay until he can be transferred to Command School. He hates being on Earth. In battle is where he belongs now.

We learn a little more about what happened behind the scenes, that Bonzo was killed, and Graff was transferred – it's unclear if he's in trouble or what. Ender will not be blamed – it was self-defense and they have it on video (kind of creepy having video cameras in a children's shower, no?). We also get further hints that the battle with the buggers is very near.

**CHAPTER THIRTEEN: "VALENTINE"** – We turn our attention back to Valentine and Peter in this chapter and learn that Graff and the others have learned the identities of "Demosthenes" and "Locke." They suspect there might be an adult coordinating them, but they can't find any evidence to support this theory. The children are simply as intelligent as Ender. They decide not to expose them for now, keeping an eye on them in case they ever get too contrary to the interests of the I.F.

Demosthenes is growing in popularity, along with Locke to a lesser degree, and Valentine enjoys the power she feels. Peter is resentful that Locke isn't more popular.

One day after school, Valentine finds Colonel Graff waiting for her. He takes her to speak with Ender, assuring her that there won't be any recording devices around. They arrive at a lake where Valentine and Ender go out on a raft he's built. They discuss what they've each been doing. He is jaded from life at Battle School, and she reminds him that he's doing it to defeat the buggers. Ender is also surprised he still cares for his sister, and that motivates him to keep going. Ender is hurt that Valentine is helping Peter to write columns, but he understands why she does it.

Ender is ready to quit. He has no confidence he can beat the buggers. Valentine tells him that he has to try, or it's his fault if the buggers win. She says, "If you try and lose then it isn't your fault. But if you don't try and we lose, then it's all your fault."

She realizes she has done exactly what Graff wanted — she made Ender decide to continue with his training and role in the attack on the buggers.

Ender and Graff leave Earth. Ender realizes that Graff is going with him wherever he goes — Ender is that important. They go to a satellite for interplanetary launches and order a space tug — a ship for hauling freight — to take them to the International Fleet's

Command center. It's on the minor planet of Eros. The tug captain is annoyed because it's about three months away, but he must submit to Graff's authority.

On the lengthy voyage, Graff gives Ender more background on the bugger situation. The I.F. is taking the offensive – they've sent ships over the eighty years since the last war, and the ships will all be arriving at the bugger homeworlds within the next five years. Also, the ships can be controlled via an *ansible* – a device that allows instantaneous communication across any distance. Graff also suspects that the buggers are capable of this as well, but their method of doing this seems to be innate to their biology. Their bodies and minds are all connected up somehow.

Because Ender want to destroy the buggers in battle, he grills Graff for any information that might help him. The buggers seem to communicate mind to mind, to not need any form of communication beyond that.

They arrive at Eros. The tug is parked at a landing platform in orbit, and a shuttle takes them to the surface of Eros, the Command center of the I.F. Ender expresses some doubt that war is the best solution, but he agrees with Graff that it's the best solution to protect humanity.

**CHAPTER FOURTEEN: "ENDER'S TEACHER"** – After their three months of travel, Ender and Graff are finally at I.F. Command on Eros. Graff inquires about his other students who are at Command, but Admiral Chamrajnagar tells him that they are not his concern.

Ender doesn't like Eros from the beginning. He finds the building design strange and unnatural. Worse, he is surrounded by people but not given a chance to really know any of them. He is given a series of teachers, but like Battle School, his real training involves a game. He will be playing a simulator, commanding a fleet in a variety of simulations. After a year of this, things change.

Ender awakes one day to find an old man sitting in his room. The man ignores Ender, but Ender is locked in the room. He does his exercises until the old man grabs his leg and knocks Ender to the floor. Later, the old man attacks him again and Ender surrenders. The old man tells Ender he is his first real teacher, because he is Ender's enemy. He says he will be programming Ender's battles in the simulator from now on.

As the old man leaves, Ender attacks him, earning a grin from the man. Ender learns that this is Mazer Rackham, the commander who won victory in the last bugger war, about eighty years ago. Ender learns that Rackham is alive because he went on a space flight – due to relativity, time passes at a different rate as you approach the speed of light. Rackham traveled through space for eight years – eight years to *him* – but fifty years passed by the time he returned to Eros. He did all this so he could train the next commander when the time for battle arrived. That next commander is Ender, the fleet's last hope. If Ender can't defeat the buggers, there will be no time to train another.

Rackham gives Ender further information about the buggers: He believes that there is a queen who controls all the others instantaneously, like they are parts of her body, and that when she is killed, the others are useless, alive in body but dead in all other respects. This is how Rackham won the first battle against the buggers. They were coming to colonize Earth and brought the queen with them. But that won't happen again, which is why Ender must reach the bugger homeworld and destroy the queen there.

It is also revealed that the Command center they are in was built by the buggers, which is why it feels so different and unnatural to Ender. Rackham then gives Ender further background on some technology in use. The main weapon is called Dr. Device, which disrupts molecules and can have a chain-reaction effect if targets are close enough together. We also hear about a defense device called the Ecstatic Shield, developed by humans but quickly adopted by the buggers.

Now that Ender is in command, he learns he will have other officers under him. To his pleasant surprise, they are the best and closest students he worked with at Battle School, including Alai, Petra, Bean, and Dink. They work together and Ender quickly improves. Rackham seems to keep changing strategy to compensate for whatever Ender learns, but Ender keeps improving. He must be distant in friendship to stay their commander, and he starts to feel a little crazy with the relentless battle schedule. While sleeping, he bites into his fist. The adults are clearly concerned for him, but they keep pushing him to win more battles.

Finally, Ender is told he is facing his final examination. Colonel Graff, Major Anderson, and others are there to watch. Ender has been having nightmares and isn't sure he can do it, but they encourage him. Ender and his team begin the battle and see that they are hopelessly outnumbered against the enemy. Their goal is to reach the homeworld, but there are enemy ships everywhere. Ender asks Mazer Rackham about using Dr. Device on the planet, and Rackham tells him he must make that decision.

Ender is eleven years old now and considers what will happen after this test – More tests? More battle and bloodshed? He is tired of it all.

When Ender and the others see the thousands of bugger ships, they are frustrated. Even the observing adults seem to think the test is unfair. Ender recalls his trick in Battle School of reaching the enemy gate. He knows he doesn't have to destroy the enemy fleet, just reach the planet. Using his small fleet as a shield, and because the buggers want to entrap him, they allow him to get close. He follows a chaotic plan and gets nearer and nearer the planet. As the enemy ships draw near him to destroy Ender's fleet, he gets as close to the planet as possible and fires Dr. Device. The planet explodes destroying most of the bugger fleet and many of Ender's ships.

Ender is sure that the adults will be angry. After all, he deliberately lost his own ships. However, the adults are overjoyed and congratulate Ender. They seem far happier than they should be. Then they tell Ender why: He hasn't been playing "games" for a long time now. All of his battle "simulations" since he met Mazer Rackham have been *real*. He has been controlling real ships light-years away with an ansible. Real ships – with real people inside them.

Tired, confused, and angry, Ender has a meltdown and stays in bed for a day. Everybody wants to congratulate him but he is sickened by what he has done, what he has become. He has been tricked and wants no more part of it.

He finally wakes and learns that there is great political upheaval on Earth. Everyone wants Ender on their side, except the Warsaw Pact, and they want Ender dead. This is a concern since there are Russian soldiers (thus tied to the Warsaw Pact) who may threaten Ender. The Polemarch (a Russian leader) has ordered Ender be killed.

Battles break out on Eros, but finally a truce is reached. We learn that the "Locke Proposal" has been accepted. Since Locke is Peter's online name, we are naturally curious what has happened. All we know at this point is that videos of Ender's victory have made him a hero everywhere. The I.F. will continue, but the Warsaw Pact will not be part of it now that the bugger threat is gone.

Ender and his friends wonder what they will do now that that war is over. They laugh at the idea of returning to regular school, to a "normal" life.

**CHAPTER FIFTEEN: "SPEAKER FOR THE DEAD"** – The war is over and Graff is at a lake. It's the same place that Ender met his sister during his brief time on Earth after Battle School. Anderson visits him and they discuss Graff's trial, in which Graff was acquitted because all his did to Ender was judged necessary to help them win the war. Anderson also testified for Graff, despite their previous differences.

They discuss Ender and why he can't come back to Earth: he's too idolized and respected, and would have too much political influence. Anderson suspects Graff knows the identity of Demosthenes. He only says that Demosthenes "explained" the Ender situation to Locke. We'll learn what this means later.

Anderson is going to be a football commissioner now that the war is over. As for Graff, he is the new Minister of Colonization. The planets left behind by the buggers will be colonized by humans, allowing the population laws to be repealed. People can now emigrate to those new worlds.

Still on Eros, Ender believes he'll be able to return to Earth eventually. He is promoted to the rank of Admiral and watches Graff's trial, learning that he did in fact kill

Stilson and Bonzo. Ender finds it curious that some people consider those two murders a crime, but not the deaths of billions of buggers. His friends all go home, but there's no word about his return to Earth.

Eros is a busy stopover as people head toward the bugger world colonies. He is a celebrity and avoids these colonists as much as possible. Then his sister arrives. Valentine is now fourteen and Ender is twelve. She is going to the first colony. Valentine tells Ender that she made sure he'd never be able to return to Earth. Peter has grown too powerful, and he would use Ender as his tool should he return. Peter has helped unite Earth to make many things possible. As they had planned, "Demosthenes" and "Locke" each rallied their supporters behind Locke's treaty, allowing peace on Earth once again. He meant to use Ender to publicly claim the power he had erected. Instead, Valentine threatened Peter with the evidence she'd amassed over the years of his cruelty. She asked Peter to leave Ender alone, and he was forced to agree.

Ender thinks Valentine is trying to control him as much as Peter, and Valentine says, "Nobody controls his own life, Ender. The best you can do is choose to fill the roles given you by good people, by people who love you." She asks Ender to go with her to the colony planet to govern. He says yes.

Valentine continues writing under the "Demosthenes" name, having informed her readers that she is heading to the colony (without identifying herself). She writes the first volume of a history of the bugger wars on the long space voyage. She also wants write Ender's biography, but Ender says there's nothing to write after the war – he hasn't done anything since. Valentine questions this.

When they finally arrive at the planet, they find things

left behind by the buggers that teach them to adapt to their new environment. The people take on a farming lifestyle.

Time passes, and Ender is now in his early twenties. A second colony ship will arrive in a year. In a helicopter, Ender and a boy named Abra go to find the best location for the new colony to build. They travel until they find an eerie place that closely resembles the video game that Ender used to play at Battle School. Ender thinks that the buggers built it for him. They knew that he was their greatest threat, and somehow looked into his mind to make this – as a marker and message. Ender doesn't let Abra go with him into the tower at "The End of the World."

He finds a room with the mirror that had always shown Peter's face. He pulls the mirror away and finds a pupa of the bugger queen, already fertilized, ready to hatch a new queen and more buggers. Ender wonders how he knows this. He feels the memories, communicated to him by the dead buggers. He also sees the wars from the perspective of the buggers, and realizes that they didn't plan a third invasion once they realized humans were sentient beings, although very different from the bugger notion of life. Ender is asked by the buggers to take the cocoon to a new planet so the buggers may be reborn. He says that humanity would kill them again in fear, but he agrees to take them through the galaxy until he finds a safe home for them.

Ender returns to his colony and writes a book told from the perspective of the bugger queen. He signs it not with his name, but with "Speaker for the Dead," and it is published. It develops a following and becomes a religion, especially popular in the colony worlds. Valentine even includes it in her history of the bugger wars. Peter Wiggin, 77 years old on Earth (because of the relativity of space travel at high speed), communicates to her that he knows it was written by Ender. Ender and Peter talk via ansible. Peter confesses everything he has done, and Ender writes his story. The two books Ender has written are called the Hive-Queen and the Hegemon.

The book ends with Ender and Valentine leaving the planet to travel the galaxy. She is known as a history writer, and he is a speaker for the dead. He takes the bugger cocoon with him, seeking a place they can live in peace.

# CRITICAL QUESTIONS & ESSAY TOPICS

Here is a list of critical questions and essay topics. These questions may be answered in a variety of ways based on your reading of the text. I have provided some suggestions for a textual response in the chapter summaries, and I encourage you to consider alternative answers as you explore these topics.

**1.** How does Ender change as he moves through different environments (Earth, Battle School, Command School) and his role changes? Is he able to control what he becomes? Similarly, how do Valentine and Peter change as they put on the online personas of "Demosthenes" and "Locke"?

**2.** Who should be accountable for the deaths of Bonzo and Stilson? Or are their deaths merely the "casualties of war"?

**3.** There is a great deal of antagonism between children and adults in the book. Are Ender and the other children ever able to overcome their manipulation by adults? What about Valentine and Peter?

**4.** A lot of the decisions about Ender's training are done not by a human, but by a computer, and a great deal of faith is put into it. Should humanity put so much trust into a computer? How does the computer's training of Ender work out?

**5.** The training at Battle School (and military installations everywhere) is harsh. Should it be less grueling? Would the students extract the same benefit and form the same bonds among themselves if it were a gentler process?

**6.** Bearing in mind that this takes place in the future and the children in this book are selected for their exceptional intelligence, do you think that they behave like children? Would an average child today behave similarly given the right circumstances?

**7.** Ender's Game can be viewed as the story of a boy sacrificing himself to help the greater whole. It can also be viewed as the story of his resistance to conformity, fighting his way out through any means necessary. What do you think the book's strongest message is?

**8.** Why do you think this book has been so popular, going beyond its original audience of young adult readers?

**9.** We see Peter alter throughout the novel. How sincere do you believe he is? Does he really want to help humanity, or is he only seeking power?

**10.** Should the adults have told Ender when he actually began to fight real battles? Do you think Ender would have performed differently in battle?

**11.** Is war justified when there is an unknown factor like the buggers – whose presence may threaten humanity – or are we obligated to seek a peaceful solution first?

# CONCLUSION

Orson Scott Card's *Ender's Game* is a classic book in the science fiction genre. It has a suspenseful story and it asks difficult questions. I hope this guide has helped you navigate this book, and deepened your understanding of all that occurs in its pages.

Made in the USA
Coppell, TX
09 August 2022

81204475R00033